hollywood cocktails

hollywood cocktails

over 200 excellent recipes

First published in 1933
This facsimile edition first published in Great Britain in 2022 by LOM ART, an imprint of
Michael O'Mara Books Limited
9 Lion Yard
Tremadoc Road
London SW4 7NQ

A CIP catalogue record for this book is available from the British Library.

Every reasonable effort has been made to acknowledge the copyright holder. Any errors or omissions
that may have occurred are inadvertent, and anyone with any copyright queries is invited to write to the
publisher, so that a full acknowledgement may be included in subsequent editions of this work.

Papers used by Michael O'Mara Books Limited are natural, recyclable products made
from wood grown in sustainable forests. The manufacturing processes conform to the
environmental regulations of the country of origin.

ISBN: 978-1-912785-90-2 in hardback print format
ISBN: 978-1-912785-91-9 in ebook format

1 2 3 4 5 6 7 8 9 10

Printed in China

www.mombooks.com

**PROUDLY SUPPORTING
ENVIRONMENTAL CHARITIES**
www.mombooks.com/we-support

MIX
Paper from
responsible sources
FSC® C020056

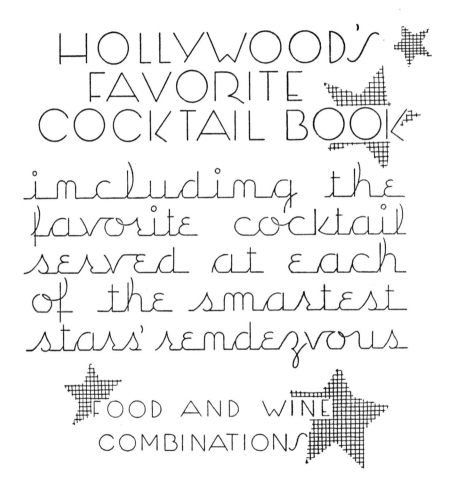

HOLLYWOOD'S FAVORITE COCKTAIL BOOK

including the favorite cocktail served at each of the smartest stars' rendezvous

FOOD AND WINE COMBINATIONS

Coconut Grove

COCONUT COCKTAIL

⅓   Italian Vermouth
⅓   French Vermouth
⅓   Dry Gin
1   Slice Pineapple

> Shake well and strain
> into cocktail glass.

ABSINTHE COCKTAIL

½ Absinthe
½ Water
1 Dash Syrup
1 Dash Angostura Bitters

Shake well and strain
into cocktail glass.

ABSINTHE (Special) COCKTAIL

⅔ Absinthe
⅙ Gin
⅙ Syrup of Anisette or Gomme Syrup
1 Dash Orange Bitters
1 Dash Angostura Bitters

Shake thoroughly and strain
into cocktail glass.

ALASKA COCKTAIL

¾ Dry Gin
¼ Yellow Chartreuse

Shake well and strain
into cocktail glass.

ALEXANDER COCKTAIL

½ Dry Gin
¼ Creme de Cacao
¼ Sweet Cream

Shake well and strain
into cocktail glass.

ANGEL FACE COCKTAIL

⅓ Dry Gin
⅓ Apricot Brandy
⅓ Calvados

Shake well and strain
into cocktail glass.

ANGEL'S KISS COCKTAIL

¼ Creme de Cacao
¼ Prunelle Brandy
¼ Creme de Violette
¼ Sweet Cream

Use liqueur glass and pour carefully,
so that ingredients do not mix.

ANGEL'S WING COCKTAIL

½ Creme de Cacao
½ Prunelle Brandy

Use liqueur glass and pour ingredients carefully, so that they do not mix. Pour a little sweet cream on top.

APPLEJACK COCKTAIL

1 Dash Angostura Bitters
½ Italian Vermouth
½ Calvados

Shake well and strain into cocktail glass.

APRICOT COCKTAIL

¼ Lemon Juice
¼ Orange Juice
½ Apricot Brandy
1 Dash Dry Gin

Shake well and strain into cocktail glass.

ARROWHEAD COCKTAIL

The White of 1 Egg
⅙ Lemon Juice
⅙ French Vermouth
⅙ Italian Vermouth
½ Canadian Club Whisky

Shake well and strain into medium-size glass.

ARTIST'S (Special) COCKTAIL

⅓ Whisky
⅙ Lemon Juice
⅓ Sherry
⅙ Groseille Syrup

Shake well and strain into cocktail glass.

ATTA BOY COCKTAIL

⅓ French Vermouth
⅔ Dry Gin
4 Dashes Grenadine

Shake well and strain into cocktail glass.

BACARDI (Special) COCKTAIL

1   Teaspoonful Grenadine
⅓   Gin
⅔   Bacardi Rum
     The Juice of ½ Lime

     Shake well and strain
     into cocktail glass.

THE BARBARY COAST COCKTAIL

¼   Gin
¼   Scotch Whisky
¼   Creme de Cacao
¼   Cream
     Cracked Ice

     Serve in a highball glass.

BEL-AIR COCKTAIL

½   Dry Gin
½   Italian Vermouth
4   Dashes Curacao

     Shake well and strain into cocktail
     glass. Squeeze lemon peel on top.

BELMONT COCKTAIL

⅓   Grenadine
⅔   Dry Gin
1   Teaspoonful Fresh Cream

     Shake well and strain
     into cocktail glass.

BETWEEN-THE-SHEETS COCKTAIL

1   Dash Lemon Juice
⅓   Brandy
⅓   Cointreau
⅓   Bacardi Rum

     Shake well and strain
     into cocktail glass.

BIFFY COCKTAIL

¼   Lemon Juice
¼   Swedish Punch
½   Dry Gin

     Shake well and strain
     into cocktail glass.

BIG BOY COCKTAIL

½ Brandy
¼ Cointreau
¼ Sirop-de-Citron

Shake well and strain
into cocktail glass.

BLOOD AND SAND COCKTAIL

¼ Orange Juice
¼ Scotch Whisky
¼ Cherry Brandy
¼ Italian Vermouth

Shake well and strain
into cocktail glass.

BLOODHOUND COCKTAIL

¼ French Vermouth
¼ Italian Vermouth
½ Dry Gin
   2 or 3 Crushed Strawberries

Shake well and strain
into cocktail glass.

BLUE BIRD COCKTAIL

4 Dashes Angostura Bitters
¾ Wineglassful of Gin
5 Dashes Orange Curacao

Shake well and strain
into cocktail glass.

BLUE DEVIL COCKTAIL

½ Dry Gin
¼ Lemon Juice or Lime Juice
¼ Maraschino
1 Dash Blue Vegetable Extract

Shake well and strain
into cocktail glass.

BLUES COCKTAIL (6 people)

   Take 4 glasses of Whisky
1 Glass of Curacao

Incorporate 1 Teaspoonful of
syrup of Prunes. Pour out over
plenty of cracked ice and shake
for longer and more thoroughly
than usual. Serve very cold.

BOMBAY COCKTAIL (No. 1)

4 Dashes Lemon Juice
¾ Wineglass East Indian Punch

Shake well and strain
into cocktail glass.

BOMBAY COCKTAIL (No. 2)

1 Dash Absinthe
2 Dashes Curacao
¼ French Vermouth
¼ Italian Vermouth
½ Brandy

Shake well and strain
into cocktail glass.

BOOMERANG COCKTAIL

1 Dash Lemon Juice
1 Dash Angostura Bitters
⅓ French Vermouth
⅓ Canadian Club Whisky
⅓ Swedish Punch

Shake well and strain
into cocktail glass.

BOSOM CARESSER COCKTAIL

The Yolk of 1 Egg
1 Teaspoonful of Grenadine
⅓ Curacao
⅔ Brandy

Shake well and strain into
medium-size glass.

BRANDY COCKTAIL

2 Dashes Curacao
¾ Wineglass Brandy

Stir well and strain into
cocktail glass.

BRANDY BLAZER COCKTAIL

Use small thick glass
1 Lump Sugar
1 Piece of Orange Peel
1 Piece of Lemon Peel
1 Glass Brandy

Light with match, stir with long
spoon for a few seconds and
strain into cocktail glass.

SARDI'S DELIGHT COCKTAIL

¼	ounce Passion Fruit Syrup
⅛	ounce Lime Juice
	A few dashes Absinthe
	A few dashes Grenadine
1	Dash Angostura Bitters
1	Good Drink Gin

Shake well.

BRANDY (Special) COCKTAIL

3 or 4 Dashes Gomme Syrup
2 or 3 Dashes Bitters
    1   Wineglass Brandy
1 or 2 Dashes Curacao

       Squeeze lemon peel;
       fill one-third full of ice,
       and stir with spoon.

BRANDY VERMOUTH COCKTAIL

1   Dash Angostura Bitters
¼   Italian Vermouth
¾   Brandy

    Stir well and strain into
    cocktail glass.

BRAZIL COCKTAIL

1   Dash Angostura Bitters
1   Dash Absinthe
½   French Vermouth
½   Sherry

    Stir well and strain into cocktail
    glass. Squeeze lemon peel on top.

BREAKFAST COCKTAIL

⅓   Grenadine
⅔   Dry Gin
    The White of 1 Egg

    Shake well and strain
    into large wine glass.

BROKEN SPUR COCKTAIL

    The Yolk of 1 Egg
⅙   Gin
⅙   Italian Vermouth
1   Teaspoonful Anisette Marie Brisard
⅔   White Port

    Shake well and strain
    into cocktail glass.

BRONX COCKTAIL

    The Juice of ¼ Orange
¼   French Vermouth
¼   Italian Vermouth
½   Dry Gin

    Shake well and strain
    into cocktail glass.

BRONX SILVER COCKTAIL

The Juice of ¼ Orange
The White of 1 Egg
¼ Italian Vermouth
¼ French Vermouth
½ Dry Gin

Shake well and strain
into large wine glass.

BULL-DOG COCKTAIL

Put 2 or 3 lumps of ice into
a large tumbler, add the juice
of 1 orange, 1 glass of gin. Fill
balance with ginger ale. Stir,
and serve with a straw.

B.V.D. COCKTAIL

⅓ Bacardi Rum
⅓ Dry Gin
⅓ French Vermouth

Shake well and strain
into cocktail glass.

CABARET COCKTAIL

1 Dash Absinthe
1 Dash Angostura Bitters
½ Dry Gin
½ Caperitif

Shake well and strain into
cocktail glass. Add a cherry.

CAFE DE PARIS COCKTAIL

The White of 1 Egg
3 Dashes Anisette
1 Teaspoonful of Fresh Cream
1 Glass Dry Gin

Shake well and strain into
medium-size glass.

CALIENTE COCKTAIL

2 Dashes Angostura Bitters
¼ Lime Juice
¾ Dry Gin

Shake well and strain
into cocktail glass.

CANADIAN COCKTAIL

The Juice of ¼ Lemon
¼ Tablespoonful Powdered Sugar
1 Liqueur Glass Curacao
3 Dashes Jamaica Rum

Shake well and strain
into cocktail glass.

CANADIAN WHISKY COCKTAIL

2 Dashes Angostura Bitters
2 Teaspoonsful Gomme Syrup
1 Glass Canadian Club Whisky

Shake well and strain
into cocktail glass.

CARMEL COCKTAIL

¼ Brandy
½ Italian Vermouth
¼ Dry Gin

Shake well and strain
into cocktail glass.

CARUSO COCKTAIL

⅓ Dry Gin
⅓ French Vermouth
⅓ Green Creme de Menthe

Shake well and strain
into cocktail glass.

CHAMPAGNE COCKTAIL

⅙ Grenadine
⅙ Cederlunds Swedish Punch
⅙ Calvados
⅙ Lemon Juice
⅓ Gin

Put into a wine glass one lump
of sugar, and saturate it with
Angostura Bitters. Having added
to this 1 lump of ice, fill the glass
with Champagne, squeeze on
top a piece of Lemon Peel, and
serve with a slice of Orange.

CHANTICLER COCKTAIL

    The Juice of ½ Lemon
1   Tablespoonful Raspberry Syrup
    The White of 1 Egg
1   Glass Dry Gin

    Shake well and strain into
    medium-size glass.

CHERRY BLOSSOM COCKTAIL (6 people)

    To a glass half full of cracked ice add a tablespoonful of dry Curacao, one of Lemon Juice, one of Grenadine, 2½ glasses of Cherry Brandy and two of Brandy. Shake thoroughly and serve very cold.

CHINATOWN COCKTAIL

1   Dash Orange Bitters
1   Dash Lemon or Lime Juice
1   Dash Brandy
⅓   Italian Vermouth
⅓   French Vermouth
⅓   Dry Gin

    Shake well and strain into cocktail glass. Squeeze Lemon Peel on top.

CHINESE COCKTAIL

1   Dash Angostura Bitters
3   Dashes Maraschino
3   Dashes Curacao
⅓   Grenadine
⅔   Jamaica Rum

    Shake well and strain into cocktail glass.

CHOKER COCKTAIL (6 people)

4   Glasses Scotch Whisky
2   Glasses Absinthe
1   Dash Absinthe Bitters

    Shake well and strain into cocktail glass.

CINZANO COCKTAIL

2   Dashes Angostura
2   Dashes Orange Bitters
1   Glass Cinzano Vermouth

    Shake well and strain into cocktail glass, and squeeze Orange Peel on top.

The Vendome

THE VENDOME COCKTAIL

⅓ Dubonnet
⅓ Gin
⅓ French Vermouth

In measuring, put a little
more Dubonnet and a
little less Vermouth.

CINZANO SPARKLING COCKTAIL

In a wineglass put 1 lump of Sugar, 2 dashes of Angostura, 1 dash of Curacao, 1 teaspoonful Brandy, 1 lump of Ice. Fill up with Cinzano Brut, and stir slightly, and squeeze lemon peel on top.

CLOVER LEAF COCKTAIL

	The Juice of ½ Lemon or of 1 Lime
⅓	Grenadine
	The White of 1 Egg
⅔	Dry Gin

Shake well and strain into medium-size glass. Put a sprig of fresh Mint on top.

CLARIDGE COCKTAIL

⅓	Dry Gin
⅓	French Vermouth
⅙	Apricot Brandy
⅙	Cointreau

Shake well and strain into cocktail glass.

COCKTAIL DAIGUIRI

1	Jigger of Bacardi
1	Teaspoon of Granulated Sugar or Sugared Syrup
	The Juice of ½ Green Lime
	Cracked Ice

Shake well. Serve frappe. Mix in order as stated above.

CLUB COCKTAIL

⅔	Dry Gin
⅓	Italian Vermouth
1	Dash Yellow Chartreuse

Shake well and strain into cocktail glass.

COFFEE COCKTAIL

	The Yolk of 1 Egg
1	Teaspoonful Sugar or Gomme Syrup
⅓	Port Wine
⅙	Brandy
1	Dash Curacao

Shake well and strain into a small wineglass, grate a little nutmeg on top.

CORDOVA COCKTAIL

⅔ Dry Gin
1 Dash Absinthe
⅓ Italian Vermouth
1 Teaspoonful Fresh Cream

Shake well and strain
into cocktail glass.

CREOLE COCKTAIL

½ Rye or Canadian Club Whisky
½ Italian Vermouth
2 Dashes Benedictine
2 Dashes Amer Picon

Stir well and strain into cocktail
glass. Twist lemon peel on top.

CORPSE REVIVER (No. 1)

¼ Italian Vermouth
¼ Apple Brandy or Calvados
½ Brandy

Shake well and strain
into cocktail glass.

CORPSE REVIVER (No. 2)

¼ Wine Glass Lemon Juice
¼ Wine Glass Kina Lillet
¼ Wine Glass Cointreau
¼ Wine Glass Dry Gin
1 Dash Absinthe

Shake well and strain
into cocktail glass.

THE COWBOY COCKTAIL

⅔ Whisky
⅓ Cream

Shake well and strain
into cocktail glass.

CUBAN COCKTAIL (No. 1)

The Juice of ¼ Lemon
1 Teaspoonful Powdered Sugar
1 Glass Bacardi Rum

Shake well and strain
into cocktail glass.

CUBAN COCKTAIL (No. 2)

The Juice of ½ Lime or ¼ Lemon
⅓   Apricot Brandy
⅔   Brandy

Shake well and strain
into cocktail glass.

CURACAO COCKTAIL (6 people)

½   Glass Brandy
2½ Glasses Dark Curacao
2½ Glasses Orange Juice
½   Glass Gin
    Broken Ice

Shake well and serve in glasses
rinsed out with orange bitters.

DAMN-THE-WEATHER COCKTAIL

3   Dashes Curacao
¼   Orange Juice
¼   Italian Vermouth
½   Dry Gin

Shake well and strain
into cocktail glass.

DEL MONTE COCKTAIL

1   Lump Sugar
    The Juice of ½ Lime or ¼ Lemon
2   Dashes Grenadine
1   Piece Orange Peel
1   Glass Canadian Club Whisky

Shake well and strain
into cocktail glass.

DEPTH BOMB COCKTAIL

1   Dash Lemon Juice
4   Dashes Grenadine
½   Calvados or Apple Brandy
½   Brandy

Shake well and strain
into cocktail glass.

DESERT HEALER COCKTAIL

The Juice of 1 Orange
1   Glass Dry Gin
½   Liqueur Glass Cherry Brandy

Shake well and strain into long
tumbler and fill with Ginger Beer.

DEVIL'S COCKTAIL

½   Port Wine
½   French Vermouth
2   Dashes Lemon Juice

Shake well and strain
into cocktail glass.

DIXIE WHISKY COCKTAIL
(6 people)

To 2 lumps of sugar, add a small
teaspoon of Angostura Bitters,
another of Lemon Juice, four glasses
of Whisky, a small teaspoonful of
Curacao, and 2 teaspoonsful of
Creme de Menthe. Add plenty
of ice and shake carefully. Serve.

DOUGLAS FAIRBANKS
COCKTAIL

⅓   French Vermouth
⅔   Plymouth Gin

Shake well and strain into
cocktail glass. Squeeze orange
and lemon peel on top.

DRY MARTINI COCKTAIL

½   French Vermouth
½   Gin
1   Dash Orange Bitters

Shake well and strain
into cocktail glass.

DUBONNET COCKTAIL

½   Dubonnet
½   Dry Gin

Stir well and strain into cocktail glass.

EAGLE'S SCREAM COCKTAIL

1   Teaspoonful of Powdered Sugar
    The White of 1 Egg
    The Juice of ¼ Lemon
¼   Creme Yvette
¾   Dry Gin

Shake well and strain into
medium-size glass.

EARTHQUAKE COCKTAIL

⅓ Gin
⅓ Scotch Whisky
⅓ Absinthe

Shake well and strain
into cocktail glass.

ELISSA LANDI COCKTAIL

Use Port Wine Glass
Fill with Shaved Ice
Fill glass ¾ full with White Creme
de Menthe and top with Brandy.

ELK'S COCKTAIL

The White of 1 Egg
½ Scotch Whisky
½ Port Wine
Juice of 1 Lemon
1 Teaspoon Sugar

Shake well and strain
into wine glass.

"EVERYTHING BUT" COCKTAIL

¼ Whisky
¼ Gin
¼ Lemon Juice
¼ Orange Juice
1 Egg
1 Teaspoonful of Apricot Brandy
Powdered Sugar

Shake well and strain
into cocktail glass.

EXTRA GIRL COCKTAIL

The Juice of ¼ Orange
⅓ Dry Gin
⅓ Italian Vermouth
⅓ French Vermouth

Shake well and strain into
medium-size glass. Add slice
of orange and cherry.

FALLEN ANGEL COCKTAIL

1   Dash Angostura Bitters
2   Dashes Creme de Menthe
    The Juice of 1 Lemon or ½ Lime
1   Glass Dry Gin

    Shake well and strain
    into cocktail glass.

FERNET BRANCA COCKTAIL
(for the morning after)

¼   Fernet Branca
¼   Italian Vermouth
½   Dry Gin

    Shake well and strain
    into cocktail glass.

FIFTY-FIFTY COCKTAIL

½   Dry Gin
½   French Vermouth

    Shake well and strain
    into cocktail glass.

FLYING SCOTCHMAN COCKTAIL
(6 people)

2½ Glasses Italian Vermouth
3   Glasses Scotch Whisky
1   Tablespoon Bitters
1   Tablespoon Sugar Syrup

    Shake well and strain
    into cocktail glass.

FOURFLUSH COCKTAIL

1   Dash Grenadine or Syrup
¼   French Vermouth
¼   Swedish Punch
½   Bacardi Rum

    Shake well and strain
    into cocktail glass.

THE FRENCH "75" COCKTAIL

⅔   Gin
⅓   Lemon Juice
1   Spoonful Powdered Sugar

    Pour into tall glass containing
    cracked ice and fill up
    with Champagne.

BROWN DERBY COCKTAIL

- ½   Whisky
- ¼   Grapefruit Juice
- ¼   Honey

    Shake well and strain
    into cocktail glass.

GARBO GARGLE COCKTAIL

1   Dash Creme de Menthe
¼   Orange Juice
¼   Grenadine
¼   French Vermouth
¼   Brandy

Shake well and strain into medium-size glass and top with a little Port Wine.

GIN COCKTAIL

4   Dashes Orange Bitters
1   Glass Dry Gin

Shake well and strain into cocktail glass.

GINGER ROGERS COCKTAIL

⅓   French Vermouth
⅓   Dry Gin
⅓   Apricot Brandy
4   Dashes Lemon Juice

Shake well and strain into cocktail glass.

GLAD EYE COCKTAIL

⅓   Peppermint
⅔   Absinthe

Shake well and strain into cocktail glass.

THE GOLDEN GATE COCKTAIL

¾   Orange Ice
¼   Gin

Place in shaker and shake, no ice.

GRAND SLAM COCKTAIL

¼   French Vermouth
¼   Italian Vermouth
½   Swedish Punch

Shake well and strain into cocktail glass.

GRAPEFRUIT COCKTAIL (6 people)

The Juice of 1½ Lemons
2   Small spoonsful Grapefruit Jelly
4   Glasses Gin

Add ice and shake.

Variation:

Take 3½ glasses of Gin and the juice of 1½ good-sized Grapefruit. Sugar to taste, plenty of ice. Shake and serve.

GYPSY COCKTAIL

½   Italian Vermouth
½   Plymouth Gin

Shake well and strain into cocktail glass.

HARRY'S (Paris) COCKTAIL

⅓   Italian Vermouth
1   Dash Absinthe
⅔   Gin
2   Sprigs Fresh Mint

Shake well and strain into cocktail glass. Serve with stuffed Olives.

HASTY COCKTAIL

1   Dash Absinthe
4   Dashes Grenadine
⅓   French Vermouth
⅔   Nicholson's Gin

Shake well and strain into cocktail glass.

HAVANA COCKTAIL

1   Dash Lemon Juice
¼   Dry Gin
¼   Swedish Punch
½   Apricot Brandy

Shake well and strain into cocktail glass.

HAWAIIAN COCKTAIL

4 Parts Gin
2 Parts Orange Juice
1 Part Curacao (or any other of the Orange Liqueurs)

Shake well and strain into cocktail glass.

HELL COCKTAIL (6 people)

Shake 3 glasses of Cognac and 3 glasses of Green Creme de Menthe. Serve with a pinch of Red Pepper on each glass.

HEY HEY COCKTAIL

¼ Lemon Juice
¼ Kina Lillet
¼ Cointreau
¼ Brandy

Shake well and strain into cocktail glass.

HONEYMOON COCKTAIL

The Juice of ½ Lemon
3 Dashes Curacao
½ Benedictine
½ Apple Brandy

Shake well and strain into cocktail glass.

HONOLULU COCKTAIL (No. 1)

1 Dash Angostura Bitters
1 Dash Orange Juice
1 Dash Pineapple Juice
1 Dash Lemon Juice
1 Glass Dry Gin
A little Powdered Sugar

Shake well and strain into cocktail glass

HONOLULU COCKTAIL (No. 2)

⅓ Maraschino
⅓ Gin
⅓ Benedictine

Shake well and strain into cocktail glass.

HURRICANE COCKTAIL

⅓ Scotch Whisky
⅓ London Dry Gin
⅓ Creme de Menthe
   Juice 2 Lemons

   Shake well and strain
   into cocktail glass.

IRISH COCKTAIL

2 Dashes Absinthe
2 Dashes Curacao
1 Dash Maraschino
1 Dash Angostura Bitters
½ Glass Irish Whisky

   Shake well and strain into
   cocktail glass. Add Olive,
   squeeze Orange Peel on top.

JACK DEMPSEY COCKTAIL

1 Dash Lemon Juice
1 Dash Syrup
¼ Bacardi Rum
¾ Dry Gin

   Shake well and strain
   into cocktail glass.

JEAN HARLOW COCKTAIL

½ Bacardi Rum
½ Italian Vermouth
   The peel of 1 Lime or
   piece of Lemon

   Shake well and strain
   into cocktail glass.

JOCKEY CLUB COCKTAIL

1 Dash Orange Bitters
1 Dash Angostura Bitters
2 Dashes Creme de Noyau
4 Dashes Lemon Juice
¾ Glass Dry Gin

   Shake well and strain
   into cocktail glass.

JOHNNIE AGGIE COCKTAIL

½ Italian Vermouth
½ Scotch Whisky
3 Dashes Benedictine

Shake well and strain into cocktail glass. Squeeze Lemon Peel on top.

JOHNNY WEISMULLER COCKTAIL

⅓ Gin
⅓ Bacardi Rum
⅓ Lemon Juice
   Powdered Sugar
1 Dash of Grenadine

Shake well and strain into cocktail glass.

LADIES' COCKTAIL

2 Dashes Absinthe
2 Dashes Anisette
2 Dashes Angostura Bitters
1 Glass of Canadian Club Whisky

Stir well and put small piece of Pineapple in glass.

LANDLADY COCKTAIL

   The White of 1 Egg
1 Tablespoonful Grenadine
1 Glass Plymouth Gin

Shake well and strain into medium-size glass.

LEE TRACY COCKTAIL

3 Dashes Absinthe
⅓ Orange Curacao
⅔ Sloe Gin

Shake well and strain into cocktail glass.

LEAVE IT TO ME COCKTAIL (No. 1)

1 Dash Lemon Juice
¼ Apricot Brandy
¼ French Vermouth
1 Dash Grenadine
½ Plymouth Gin

Shake well and strain into cocktail glass.

LEAVE IT TO ME COCKTAIL (No. 2)

1   Teaspoonful Raspberry Syrup
1   Teaspoonful Lemon Juice
1   Dash Maraschino
¾   Glass Dry Gin

Shake well and strain
into cocktail glass.

LIAR'S COCKTAIL

6   Dashes Curacao
2   Dashes Italian Vermouth
⅓   French Vermouth
⅔   Dry Gin

Shake well and strain
into cocktail glass.

LINDBERGH COCKTAIL

2   Dashes Orange Juice
2   Dashes Pricota
½   Kina Lillet
½   Plymouth Gin

Shake well and serve in cocktail
glass. Squeeze Lemon Peel on top.

LOS ANGELES COCKTAIL

The Juice of 1 Lemon
4   Hookers Whisky
4   Teaspoonsful Sugar
1   Egg
1   Dash Italian Vermouth

Shake well and strain
into cocktail glass.

LOUD SPEAKER COCKTAIL

⅛   Lemon Juice
⅛   Cointreau
⅜   Dry Gin
⅜   Brandy

Shake well and strain
into cocktail glass.

LUPE VELEZ COCKTAIL (6 people)

3   Glasses Jamaica Rum
1½   Glasses Kummel
1½   Glasses Orange Juice
1   Dash Pimento Dram

Shake carefully and serve
whilst frothing.

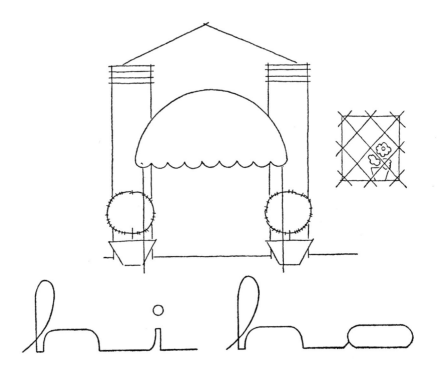

HI HO COCKTAIL

2	Dashes Orange Bitters
⅓	Port Wine
⅔	Tom Gin

Stir well and strain into cocktail glass. Squeeze Lemon Peel on top.

MAE WEST COCKTAIL

    The Yolk of 1 Egg
1   Teaspoonful Powdered Sugar
1   Glass Brandy

    Shake well and strain into
    medium-size glass. Dash of
    Cayenne Pepper on top.

MAIDEN'S PRAYER COCKTAIL (No. 1)

⅛   Orange Juice
⅛   Lemon Juice
⅜   Cointreau
⅜   Dry Gin

    Shake well and strain
    into cocktail glass.

MAIDEN'S PRAYER COCKTAIL (No. 2)

⅓   Kina Lillet
⅓   Dry Gin
⅙   Calvados
⅙   Apricot Brandy

    Shake well and strain
    into cocktail glass.

MARLENE DIETRICH COCKTAIL

¾   Wineglass Rye or Canadian Whisky
2   Dashes Angostura Bitters
2   Dashes Curacao

    Shake well and strain into
    wineglass. Squeeze Lemon
    and Orange Peel on top.

MARTINI (Dry) COCKTAIL

⅓   French Vermouth
⅔   Dry Gin

    Shake well and strain
    into cocktail glass.

MALIBU COCKTAIL

⅓   Cointreau
⅓   Anisette
⅓   White Curacao

    Shake well and strain
    into cocktail glass.

MANHATTAN COCKTAIL (No. 1)

Use small Bar Glass

2   Dashes Curacao or Maraschino
1   Rye Whisky
1   Wineglass Vermouth (mixed)
3   Dashes Angostura Bitters
2   Small lumps of Ice

Shake up well, and strain into a claret glass. Put a quarter of a slice of Lemon in the glass and serve. If preferred very sweet add two dashes of gum syrup.

MANHATTAN COCKTAIL (No. 2)

1   Dash Angostura Bitters
⅔   Canadian Club Whisky
⅓   Italian Vermouth

Shake well and strain into cocktail glass, with cherry.

MANHATTAN COCKTAIL DRY

¼   French Vermouth
¼   Italian Vermouth
½   Rye or Canadian Club Whisky

Stir well and strain into cocktail glass.

MARTINI (Medium) COCKTAIL

¼   French Vermouth
¼   Italian Vermouth
½   Dry Gin

Shake well and strain into cocktail glass.

MARTINI (Special) COCKTAIL (6 people)

4   Glasses of Gin
1½ Glasses Italian Vermouth
⅓   Glass Orange-Flower Water

Before shaking, add a dash of Absinthe and 1 or 2 dashes of Angostura Bitters.

MARY PICKFORD COCKTAIL

½   Bacardi Rum
½   Pineapple Juice
1   Teaspoonful Grenadine
6   Drops Maraschino

Shake well and strain
into cocktail glass.

MAX BAER COCKTAIL

2   Dashes Absinthe
2   Dashes Grenadine
½   Gin
½   Calvados

Shake well and strain
into cocktail glass.

MERRY WIDOW COCKTAIL

2   Dashes Absinthe
2   Dashes Angostura Bitters
2   Dashes Benedictine
½   French Vermouth
½   Dry Gin

Stir well and strain into cocktail
glass. Twist Lemon Peel on top.

MINT COCKTAIL (6 people)

Soak a few sprigs of fresh mint
for two hours in a glass and a half
of White Wine. Add half a glass
of Creme de Menthe, 2 glasses
of Gin, and 1½ glasses of White
Wine. Ice, and shake thoroughly.
Serve with a sprig of mint
tastefully arranged in each glass.

MINT JULEP

Put into tumbler a dozen sprigs
of tender mint shoots. Upon
them pour one spoonful white
sugar. Fill to one-third with
Brandy. Fill up tumbler then
with fine ice. Add dash of rum
of peppermint. As the ice melts
you drink. (Bourbon whisky may
be substituted for brandy.)

MONKEY GLAND COCKTAIL

3 Dashes Absinthe
3 Dashes Grenadine
⅓ Orange Juice
⅔ Dry Gin

Shake well and strain
into cocktail glass.

MOONSHINE COCKTAIL
(6 people)

3 Glasses Gin
2 Glasses French Vermouth
1 Glass Maraschino

Before shaking add a drop
of Absinthe Bitters.

MOVIE LOT COCKTAIL

⅓ Grape Juice
⅓ Swedish Punch
⅓ Dry Gin

Shake well and strain
into cocktail glass.

NEW ORLEANS FIZZ

  Juice of ½ Lemon
½ Tablespoon Powdered Sugar
  White of 1 Egg
1 Glass Dry Gin
3 Dashes Fleur d'Orange
1 Tablespoon Sweet Cream

Long tumbler. Shake well
and strain into glass. Fill with
Rosa Blanca or Seltzer.

OLD-FASHIONED COCKTAIL

1 Lump Sugar
2 Dashes Angostura Bitters
1 Glass Rye or Canadian Club Whisky

Crush Sugar and Bitters together,
add lump of ice, decorate with
twist of lemon peel and slice of
orange, using medium-size glass,
and stir well. This Cocktail can
be made with Brandy, Gin, Rum,
etc., instead of Rye Whisky.

NIGHT CAP COCKTAIL

The Yolk of 1 Egg
⅓ Anisette
⅓ Curacao
⅓ Brandy

Shake well and strain
into cocktail glass.

"OLD PAL" COCKTAIL

⅓ Canadian Club Whisky
⅓ French Vermouth
⅓ Campari

Shake well and strain
into cocktail glass.

ORANGE BLOSSOM COCKTAIL

½ Orange Juice
½ Dry Gin

Shake well and strain
into cocktail glass.

PALM SPRINGS COCKTAIL

1 Dash Angostura Bitters
1 Dash Orange Bitters
⅓ Creme de Cacao
⅓ Maraschino
⅓ French Vermouth

Shake well and strain
into cocktail glass.

PANAMA COCKTAIL

⅓ Creme de Cacao
⅓ Sweet Cream
⅓ Brandy

Shake well and strain
into cocktail glass.

PARADISE COCKTAIL

1 Dash Lemon Juice
¼ Orange Juice
½ Gin
¼ Apricot Brandy

Shake well and strain
into cocktail glass.

PEGU CLUB COCKTAIL

1   Dash Angostura Bitters
1   Dash Orange Bitters
1   Teaspoon Lime Juice
⅓   Curacao
⅔   Dry Gin

Shake well, strain into cocktail glass.

PINEAPPLE COCKTAIL
(6 people)

First take a glass of fresh pineapple juice. Soak the fruit from which this juice has been extracted for two hours in two glasses of Dry White Wine. Mix these together, adding as well the juice of a quarter of a Lemon, and pour the whole into the shaker with 3 glasses of Sherry. Stand the shaker in ice, but do not put any ice into the mixture. Shake, strain, and serve with a small piece of pineapple in the glass. This is a very mild cocktail.

PLAIN VERMOUTH COCKTAIL
(6 people)

5½   Glasses French Vermouth
1   Teaspoonful Absinthe Bitters
1   Teaspoonful Maraschino

Shake very thoroughly and serve with a cherry.

PLAZA PICK-ME-UP COCKTAIL

The Yolk of 1 Egg
1   Glass Brandy
1   Teaspoonful Castor Sugar

Shake well and strain into medium-size wine glass and fill balance with Ayala Champagne.

POLO COCKTAIL (No. 1)

The Juice of ¼ or ½ Lime
⅓   Italian Vermouth
⅓   French Vermouth
⅓   Dry Gin

Shake well and strain into cocktail glass.

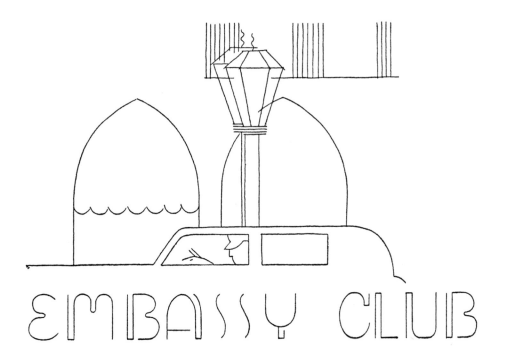

EMBASSY COCKTAIL

¼ Brandy
¼ Cointreau
¼ Jamaica Rum
¼ Lime

Shake well and strain
into cocktail glass.

POLO COCKTAIL (No. 2)

⅙   Grapefruit Juice
⅙   Orange Juice
⅔   Plymouth Gin

Shake well and strain
into cocktail glass.

POOP-POOP-A-DOOP COCKTAIL

⅓   Bacardi Rum
1   Dash Apricot Brandy
⅓   Swedish Punch
⅓   Dry Gin

Shake well and strain
into cocktail glass.

PRAIRIE OYSTER COCKTAIL

2   Dashes Vinegar
     The Yolk of 1 Egg
1   Teaspoonful Worchestershire Sauce
1   Teaspoonful Tomato Catsup
1   Dash of Pepper on top

Do not break the Yolk of Egg.

RACQUET CLUB COCKTAIL

1   Dash Orange Bitters
⅓   French Vermouth
⅔   Plymouth Gin

Shake well and strain
into cocktail glass.

RATTLESNAKE COCKTAIL (6 people)

4   Glasses Rye Whisky
     The Whites of 2 Eggs
1   Glass Sweetened Lemon Juice
     A few dashes Absinthe

Shake very thoroughly; serve by
straining it through a fine sieve.

ROCK AND RYE COCKTAIL

1   Glass Rye Whisky or Canadian Club
     Dissolve 1 piece Rock Candy in it

The Juice of 1 Lemon can
be added if desired.

ROLLS ROYCE COCKTAIL

1   Dash Benedictine
¼   French Vermouth
¼   Italian Vermouth
½   Dry Gin

Shake well and strain
into cocktail glass.

ROSCOE TURNER COCKTAIL

⅓   Lemon Juice
⅔   Dry Gin
2   Dashes Maraschino

Shake well and strain
into cocktail glass.

ROULETTE COCKTAIL

¼   Swedish Punch
¼   Bacardi Rum
½   Calvados

Shake well and strain
into cocktail glass.

ROYAL COCKTAIL (No. 1)

The Juice of ½ Lemon
½   Tablespoonful Powdered Sugar
1   Egg
1   Glass Dry Gin

Shake well and strain into
medium-size glass.

ROYAL COCKTAIL (No. 2)

⅓   French Vermouth
⅓   Dry Gin
⅓   Cherry Brandy

Stir well and strain into
cocktail glass.

ROYAL COCKTAIL (No. 3)

⅓   Gin
⅓   French Vermouth
⅓   Cherry Brandy
1   Dash Maraschino

Shake well and strain into
cocktail glass, with cherry.

RUSSIAN COCKTAIL

⅓   Creme de Cacao
⅓   Dry Gin
⅓   Vodka

Shake well, strain into cocktail
glass, and tossitoff quickski.

RYE WHISKY COCKTAIL

1   Dash Angostura Bitters
4   Dashes Syrup
1   Glass Rye or Canadian Club Whisky

Stir well and strain into cocktail
glass. Add 1 cherry.

SANTA BARBARA COCKTAIL

¼   Fresh Cream
¼   Creme de Cacao
½   Vodka

Shake well and strain
into cocktail glass.

SAN DIEGO COCKTAIL

1   Dash Angostura Bitters
3   Dashes Curacao
½   Caperitif
½   Canadian Club Whisky

Stir well and strain into cocktail
glass. Lemon peel on top.

SAN FRANCISCO BUCK COCKTAIL

1   Lump of Ice
1   Glass Dry Gin
     The Juice of ½ Lemon
1   Split of Ginger Ale

Use long tumbler.

SATAN'S WHISKERS COCKTAIL (Straight)

Of Italian Vermouth, French
Vermouth, Gin and Orange
Juice, 2 parts of each; of Grand
Marnier 1 part; Orange Bitters
a dash. Shake well and
strain into cocktail glass.

SATAN'S WHISKERS COCKTAIL (Curled)

Substitute the same quantity of Orange Curacao for the Grand Marnier in the preceding. Shake well and strain into cocktail glass.

SAZERAC COCKTAIL

1   Lump of Sugar
1   Dash Angostura or Peychana Bitters
1   Glass Rye or Canadian Club Whisky

Stir well and strain into another glass that has been cooled. Add 1 dash Absinthe and squeeze Lemon Peel on top.

SHANGHAI COCKTAIL

2   Dashes Grenadine
³⁄₈ Lemon Juice
⅛   Anisette
½   Jamaica Rum

Shake well and strain into cocktail glass.

SHERRY COCKTAIL

4   Dashes Orange Bitters
4   Dashes French Vermouth
1   Glass Sherry

Stir well and strain into cocktail glass.

SIDECAR COCKTAIL

¼   Lemon Juice
¼   Cointreau
½   Brandy

Shake well and strain into cocktail glass.

SILVER COCKTAIL

2   Dashes Maraschino
2   Dashes Orange Bitters
½   French Vermouth
½   Dry Gin

Shake well and strain into cocktail glass.

MONTMARTRE (Special) COCKTAIL

2/3 Bacardi
1/3 Sweet Cream
1   Dash of Grenadine

Shake well and strain
into cocktail glass.

SINGAPORE GIN SLING

    Juice ¼ Lemon
¼ Dry Gin
2 Dashes Cherry Brandy

Shake well and strain into a medium glass. Fill with Roca Blanca water. Add one lump ice.

SCHNOZZLE DURANTE COCKTAIL (6 people)

In a shaker filled with cracked ice place a spoonful of Curacao, 2 glasses of Gin, 2 glasses of Sherry, 2 glasses of French Vermouth. Stir thoroughly with a spoon, shake, strain, and serve. Add an olive and two dashes of Absinthe to each glass.

SLOE GIN COCKTAIL

¼ French Vermouth
¼ Italian Vermouth
½ Sloe Gin

Stir well and strain into cocktail glass.

SO-AND-SO COCKTAIL

⅙ Grenadine
⅙ Calvados
⅓ Italian Vermouth
⅓ Dry Gin

Shake well and strain into cocktail glass.

SOUL KISS COCKTAIL (No. 1)

⅙ Orange Juice
⅙ Dubonnet
⅓ French Vermouth
⅓ Italian Vermouth

Shake well and strain into cocktail glass.

SOUL KISS COCKTAIL (No. 2)

⅙ Orange Juice
⅙ Dubonnet
⅓ French Vermouth
⅓ Canadian Club Whisky
1 Slice Orange

Shake well and strain into cocktail glass.

SUDDEN DEATH COCKTAIL

Juice of ¼ Lemon
1 Dash Jamaica Ginger
1 Teaspoonful Rock Candy Syrup
1 Teaspoonful Ginger Brandy
1 Glass Canadian Club Whisky

Stir well and strain into cocktail glass, but do not ice.

THE SUNRISE COCKTAIL

1 Jigger Tequila
½ Lime, squeezed, insert peel
6 Dashes Grenadine
2 Dashes Creme de Cassis
2 Lumps Ice

Serve in highball glass filled to brim with Roca Blanca water or fizz with seltzer. Stir slightly.

SYLVIA DEE COCKTAIL

1 Dash Absinthe
½ Brandy
½ Dubonnet

Shake well and strain into cocktail glass.

SWEET PATOTIE COCKTAIL

¼ Orange Juice
¼ Cointreau
½ Dry Gin

Shake well and strain into cocktail glass.

TEMPTATION COCKTAIL

1 Piece Orange Peel
1 Piece Lemon Peel
2 Dashes Dubonnet
2 Dashes Absinthe
2 Dashes Curacao
1 Glass Canadian Club Whisky

Shake well and strain into cocktail glass.

T.N.T. COCKTAIL

½ Canadian Club Whisky
½ Absinthe

Shake well and strain into cocktail glass.

TOM AND JERRY COCKTAIL

1   Egg
½   Glass Jamaica Rum
1   Tablespoonful Powdered Sugar
½   Glass Brandy

Beat up yolk and white of egg separately. Then mix the yolk and white together. Use stem glass or china mug, adding the spirits, then fill with boiling water, grating nutmeg on top.

TWIN SIX COCKTAIL

1   Dash Grenadine
4   Dashes Orange Juice
     White of 1 Egg
¼   Italian Vermouth
¾   Dry Gin

Shake well and strain into medium-size glass.

VALENCIA COCKTAIL

4   Dashes Orange Bitters
⅓   Orange Juice
⅔   Apricot Brandy

Shake well, strain into mediumsize glass, and fill with Champagne.

VAN GORDER COCKTAIL

1   Dash Absinthe
⅓   Curacao
⅔   Sloe Gin

Shake well and strain into cocktail glass.

VERMOUTH COCKTAIL

1   Glass Italian or French Vermouth
4   Dashes Orange or 1 dash Angostura Bitters

Stir well and strain into cocktail glass.

VERMOUTH AND CURACAO COCKTAIL

1 Glass French Vermouth
½ Liqueur Glass Curacao

Use medium-size glass and fill with soda water.

WEDDING BELLE COCKTAIL

⅙ Orange Juice
⅙ Cherry Brandy
⅓ Dry Gin
⅓ Dubonnet

Shake well and strain into cocktail glass.

WELCOME STRANGER COCKTAIL

⅙ Grenadine
⅙ Lemon Juice
⅙ Orange Juice
⅙ Gin
⅙ Cederlunds Punch
⅙ Brandy

Shake well and strain into cocktail glass.

WHIP COCKTAIL

1 Dash Absinthe
3 Dashes Curacao
¼ French Vermouth
¼ Italian Vermouth
½ Brandy

Shake well and strain into cocktail glass.

WHISKY COCKTAIL

1 Dash Angostura Bitters
4 Dashes Syrup
1 Glass Canadian Club Whisky

Stir well and strain into cocktail glass. Add a cherry.

WHISKY SPECIAL COCKTAIL (6 people)

3 Glasses Whisky
2 Glasses French Vermouth
½ Glass Orange Juice

Pour into the shaker and shake, adding a little nutmeg. Serve with an olive. This is a very dry cocktail.

WHISPER COCKTAIL (6 people)

2   Glasses Whisky
2   Glasses French Vermouth
2   Glasses Italian Vermouth

Pour into shaker half full of cracked ice. Shake well and serve.

WILD WEST COCKTAIL

1   Dash Lemon Juice
¼   Bacardi Rum
¾   East India Punch

Shake well and strain into cocktail glass.

WILL ROGERS COCKTAIL

¼   Orange Juice
¼   French Vermouth
½   Plymouth Gin
4   Dashes Curacao

Shake well and strain into cocktail glass.

WILSHIRE BOULEVARD COCKTAIL

⅓   Creme de Cacao
⅓   Apricot Brandy
⅓   Sweet Cream

Use liqueur glass and pour carefully, so that ingredients do not mix.

WHIZ-BANG COCKTAIL

2   Dashes Absinthe
2   Dashes Grenadine
2   Dashes Orange Bitters
⅓   French Vermouth
⅔   Scotch Whisky

Shake well and strain into cocktail glass.

YALE COCKTAIL

3   Dashes Orange Bitters
1   Dash Angostura Bitters
1   Glass Dry Gin

Shake well and strain into a small glass. Add a little syphon and squeeze Lemon Peel on top.

YELLOW RATTLER COCKTAIL

¼ Orange Juice
¼ French Vermouth
¼ Italian Vermouth
¼ Dry Gin

Shake well and strain into
cocktail glass, and serve with
small crushed pickled onion.

ZANZIBAR COCKTAIL
(6 people)

The Juice of 1½ Lemons
1 Glass Gin
3 Glasses French Vermouth
1 or 2 Dessert spoonsful Sugar Syrup

If desired, 1 spoonful Orange
Bitters. Shake well and serve
with a piece of lemon rind.

ZAZARAC COCKTAIL

⅙ Bacardi Rum
⅙ Anisette
⅙ Gomme Syrup
⅓ Canadian Club Whisky
1 Dash Angostura Bitters
1 Dash Orange Bitters
3 Dashes Absinthe

Shake well and strain into cocktail
glass. Squeeze Lemon Peel on top.

XYZ COCKTAIL

¼ Lemon Juice
¼ Cointreau
½ Bacardi Rum

Shake well and strain
into cocktail glass.

PRESIDENT ROOSEVELT
COCKTAIL

2   Dashes Grenadine
     Juice of ¼ Orange
1   Glass Bacardi Rum

     Shake well and strain
     into cocktail glass.

ROOSEVELT

food and wine combinations

TYPE OF WINE IN GASTRNOMIC SEQUENCE	SOME BETTER-KNOWN VINTAGES	GOOD RECENT YEARS
DRY DRY WHITE BURGUNDY	Chablis Pouilly Meursault Charmes	1906 1911 1915 1923 1926 1928
ALSATIAN WINES	Riquewihr Traminer	1924 1928
DEMI-SEC DEMI-SEC WHITE BURGUNDY	Montrachet Puligny Goutte d'Or	1906 1911 1916 1923 1928
LIGHT WHITE BORDEAUX	Graves, and the less liquorous Sauternes and Barsac	1904 1908 1914 1919 1923

GOURMETS
when and how to serve them

HARMONIOUS DISHES	SERVING TEMPERATURE	TYPE OF GLASS	CHARACTERISTICS
Oysters and Clams, Lobsters and Shell fish Grilled or Cold Trout, Sole, Salmon, and other fish simply prepared or grilled. Eggs, Cold Ham, Galantine, Shrimps	COLD CAVE TEMPER-ATURE	Medium tulip or spheroid with stem	Crystal clear and pale yellow . . . dry, slightly acid, with exquisite bouquet.
	VERY COLD	Long stem pale green	Very dry, fruity and aromatic. Often lacks body.
Sweetbreads . . . Paté de Foie Gras . . . Vol au Vent, Patties. Lobster Newburg, Sole Normandie and other fish dishes with a seasoned sauce. . . . Chicken with rice, Sauté, Marengo . . . Ham with Madére Sauce.	COLD CAVE TEMPER-ATURE	Large tulip or spheroid	Transparent, pale lemon gold in color. Rich, savorous and fragrant . . .
	SLIGHTLY ICED	Large tulip or spheroid	Subtle, unctuous, half-dry, perfumed wines. Light amber in color. Best when 10 or 15 years old.

TYPE OF WINE IN GASTRNOMIC SEQUENCE	SOME BETTER-KNOWN VINTAGES	GOOD RECENT YEARS
LIGHT REDS RED BORDEAUX (CLARET)	CHATEAUX: Lafite Latour Haut-Brion Ausone Léoville-Barton Ducru-Beaucaillou Rauzan-ségla	1900 1904 1911 1914 1920 1924 1928
COTES DU RHONE	Chateauneuf-du-Pape Hermitage	1923 1926 1928
HEAVY REDS RED BURGUNDY	Clos Vougeot Chambertin Romanée-Conti Richebourg Corton Hospices deBeaune Volnay	1904 1911 1915 1923 1926 1928

GOURMETS
when and how to serve them

HARMONIOUS DISHES	SERVING TEMPERATURE	TYPE OF GLASS	CHARACTERISTICS
ROAST: Duck, quail, chicken, pheasant, pigeon and turkey . . . VEAL: Roast, chops, cutlet, liver . . . LAMB: Chops, cutlets, saddle, roast leg . . . SMALL GAME: Lark, grouse, partridge. NUTS, and above all: CHEESE.	FULL ROOM TEMPER-ATURE	Very Large tulip or spheroid	Glorious red-brown in color . . . suave, delicately perfumed . . . Full, exquisite body . . . yet rarely heady, it ages best of all wines. Old bottles should be decanted and briefly exposed to the air.
	ROOM TEMPER-ATURE	Very Large tulip or spheroid	Eloquent, sun-soaked wine, the color of purple sunsets. Heady and voluptuous.
BEEF: Roast, steak, ragout, a la mode . . . MUTTON: Chops or roast . . . Wild duck, Goose, Rabbit, Hare, Venison, Wild Game, Snails and Cheese!!	ROOM TEMPER-ATURE OR SLIGHTLY LOWER	Largest of all Tulip or spheroid	Deep, fruity crimson in color. A robust, opulent, melodious wine, with heavy aroma and full body. Heady and warming. Excellent when aged 10 to 15 years.

CHART FOR
Types of wine and ....

	TYPE OF WINE IN GASTRNOMIC SEQUENCE	SOME BETTER-KNOWN VINTAGES	GOOD RECENT YEARS
DESSERT WINES	HEAVY WHITE BORDEAUX	CHATEAUX: Yquem Climens Guiraud Vigneau	1900 1901 1904 1908 1921 1924
	VOUVRAY ANJOU (WHITE)	Chateau Moncontour Coulée-de-Serrant Quarts-de-Chaume	1917 1921 1924
	CHAMPAGNE	Roederer Pol Roger Cliquot Pommery Heidsieck	1904 1906 1911 1915 1919 1923

G O U R M E T S
when and how to serve them

HARMONIOUS DISHES	SERVING TEMPERATURE	TYPE OF GLASS	CHARACTERISTICS
Poularde-sauce supreme, Lobster a l'Armoricaine Bouillabaisse Sweetbreads, and DESSERTS: Fruits, ices, pastries . . . puddings, crepes.	ICED	Large tulip or spheroid	Rich, golden, lanquorous, liquorous wines. A delight to initiates and epicures alike . . .
	COLD CAVE TEMPERATURE	Large tulip or spheroid	Clear, amber wines, with a faint natural sparkle and a gorgeous, seductive aroma. Poor travelers. Do not ice.
For: Festivity, Toasts and After-Dinner Speeches. Weddings and Divorces.	WELL ICED	Coupe, flute or tulip.	Gay, pale, sparkling wine of varied degrees of dryness, from doux to brout. The world's standard for festivity.

THE MORNING AFTER

1. **Tequila Sunrise.**
2. **Good Old Pilsener (Urquel preferred).** It cools the pipes.
3. **Clam Broth (Hot) two bowls. Rectifies the stomach.**
4. **Pick-Me-Up. Dash absinthe.**
5. **Gin Fizz (Silver or New Orleans).** Helpful to some.
6. **Tomato Juice.** Only if others are not available.

60